In the Country of Hard Life and Rosebuds

In the Country of Hard Life and Rosebuds

ANNA LEIGH KNOWLES

LOST HORSE PRESS
Liberty Lake, Washington

ACKNOWLEDGMENTS

Thank you to the editors at the following literary journals and magazines in which the following poems first appeared, sometimes under different titles:

About Place Journal: "My Great-Grandmother Crosses the River"
Louisville Review: "To the Ohio River Valley"
Nashville Review: "Country Music Show"
Nimrod International Journal: "Cooking Lessons"
Ocean State Review: "Interior Lives"
Once A City Said: A Louisville Poets Anthology: "Roses in the Eyes," "Oblivious to the Thorns," "After Everyone Is Gone," "When My Sister Told Me to Let Her Alone," and "The Past Doesn't Burst into Song Like It Used to"
storySouth: "Opossum Gossip"
Tampa Review: "In the Country of Hard Life and Rosebuds"

"Check's Almost Every Night" was awarded second place in the 2021 W.B. Yeats Poetry Award.

For their encouragement in writing this book I give my deepest gratitude to my family, particularly my sister, without whom many of these poems would be absent or unfinished. Thank you to my husband, Graham, for the time and encouragement to sit down and work. To my friends and colleagues for their annual support, especially Andrew Hemmert and John McCarthy, who helped me re-see, revise, and reshape the framework of this book. Thank you to Joy Priest for including some of these poems in *Once A City Said, A Louisville Poets' Anthology* and for the gift of community. Many thanks to the Appalachian Writers' Workshop for the scholarship to sit with these poems for a bit longer, and to Nickole Brown for talking me through several iterations of these poems. Thank you to Luke Hankins for the keen eyes and expertise in working with these earlier drafts. Many thanks to Roy Bentley and Christine Holbert for the phone call and for their ongoing belief in me. To whatever soft thread has kept me tethered to the doorways of Louisville, thank you.

Cover art: "Rosebud" by Tyler Varsell, whose work can be viewed at www.tylervarsell.com.
Author Photo: Graham Brewer.
Book Design: Christine Holbert.

FIRST EDITION

This and other Lost Horse Press titles may be purchased online at www.losthorsepress.org.

Library of Congress Cataloging-in-Publication Data may be obtained directly from the Library of Congress.

ISBN 979-8-9890965-0-3

TABLE OF CONTENTS

V

I

ROSES IN THE EYES, OBLIVIOUS TO THE THORNS

Here is a family lined up like a jury.
  Behind the peeling garage, red letters

scrawl over a white sash that spells
  Kentucky. Behind that sash

my uncle clutches the silk corner,
  smiling at it like a baptized

baby. Another scrap of sash tails off
  as my grandmother raises the edge

enough to read *Derby*. She shakes
  it back and forth. My mother is nearby

in loose jeans, sweater ruffled as clay
  mudflats. Bangs curled inward

like a hand on a steering wheel.
  My father sits in front, banners

flap over his head.
  He is a jean scarecrow

out of place for Kentucky spring.
  What do I do with the photo's whispering?

I've held it too much and each time,
  they all live the same hundred lives.

I've slept in its stasis, folded beneath
  my pillow as though it would hatch.

No one speaks, usually. Facts blur
       into fantasy. But today, they live

inside a season of wishful thinking
       stretching on and on. All they want

is to win—to jockey each eager gamble
       into one plea: *It can be.* Wagers scatter

around years swirling into focus.
       Laverne's skirt is hard to make out

in the sun cutting through the chastened
       syringa, what runs there—stitched horses

in different strides circle the hem. Me,
       not yet whole-bodied, yet to cash-in

on May's plump prize. The years
       are slow to pass, heavy-set. In the distant

future—the face of a girl who gawks
       at others, a gleaming shard, a self

calling across aphids. No matter the roses
       in the eyes, oblivious to the thorns.

HOWLING HOSTS OF EARTH

One-armed George couldn't hear a whistle
        if it sat him up in screams. It was George or Joe,

we don't know. No one knows the real story.
I just say my great uncle lost his arm up on the tracks.

Don't recall the direction of wind
        or time of year, but it was when the day trains came
        through Fallsburg so little more than a gap-tooth

of light was involved for sure. Call it June.
A familiar man drunk as a lord under the sun's
        thumbed udder. A tenant farmer

with a second grade education. His mother died
a week before he married Mary Geisler. Mary and Joseph—
        maybe those were their names.

In 1932, he had an altercation
        with a drunk in the West End of Louisville. Threat

of a knife's blunt edge on 15th and Main. My grandfather
        thinks it had to do with Mary, his mother, women

in general. Somewhere down by the docks,
I suppose. He stuck to the river out in Fallsburg

after that. Catholics followed the water, I'm told.
        Didn't cause trouble, but nursed a grudge
        for a good while. Never quit drinking, either.

Most of us still can't. He understood nothing
of the hearts choked flue but sustained its prod
and char. We use him as an example now.

Don't be like him.
Don't wander too far up.

Where crows bathed waiting for the stock-still
                    moon, his tracks peppered clover & crushed
redroot burst ember eyes. But all this was after he lost

his arm, after he fell asleep up there on the tracks. He left
the afternoon to the goldenrods heavy with monarchs

in the cricket-stitched light. A smolder of embers
whisked inland like a triple mast skirling down and out
                    the valley's edge—that's how he left us.

                    .

Prime in my years, I'm answering
for the call of day trains and one-armed George up on the tracks
                    guarded by bitter angels.

Know I'm still looking for him here, how the better things
          in me stay up each night as the dead tap their ghost-glass
& take long breaths mottling

the reeds' buckled structures. He's out there,

hidden in the blur of winter acreage and the early
          province of summer. He's out there, pushing life

toward my lips with his one arm. Just a myth
in a storyline that has changed so many times
we can't remember his name. Offer me a signal,

set me adrift. Give me some news, stargazer—
I cannot see what halogen-bright horizon
                    you crawled into. You live, legend

has it, hobbling through the underbrush unseen
                    and hurt. No last words to face the howling
hosts of earth. But I cannot find you out here

among the shawl of dark clouds shuffling off
            drawing me down a quarter mile of gingkoes
                    spread south to the family shed, wind rattling

in the eaves with the clamor of doves. Walk
                            away from this & it's just me

                            drifting in these fields,

                            just me calling you up

                            from dirt & clod & ditch.

PIG-HEARTED MAN

Winter of '94 Uncle swore
his heart was replaced with a pig's,

strutted around our kitchen
with his torso exposed

so I could see where surgeons
split the rawhide of his chest.

Seemed like good news walking,
all right. We all needed a man

with a strong voice and a little
pig in him. Uncle moved

in like a heatwave, with a temper
sharp enough to whip blooms

from cacti. He wore toy necklaces
and napped in a cardboard crown

as I pinned barrettes to his sleeves
like epaulets. I kept my own small

amazes: his gambling tokens
tucked into my overalls for luck.

Bellagio and Caesars Palace worn
smooth as margarine. He carried green

gemstones in his pockets for good
fortune. I did too. We believed in crystals

and coins more than ourselves,
though no fortune ever came

and our luck never changed
for the best. Evenings were a tease

of blue watching the Tarheels
shoot. I didn't want to leave him alone

with his rough sports. Those tense hours
under the basement I studied him—

the distance he kept between me
and the glow of TV. I was safe enough

to trust, so was he. Derby Day
we watched faded apparitions bray

states away, homesick for the honey
locust groves and cockleburs

of Kentucky. Weekends we packed
up his truck and drove toward the sand

dunes while I cranked
down the windows and hollered

toward a beveled blue-line
horizon, hundreds of miles away.

The man taught me when drifting
is in order, to grin and bear it out.

So I sidled in, bellied-down
through rug burns to the screen door

where I listened for the clatter
and shock of his Ranger, whatever

disappeared over the ridges
was my guessing game, my escape plan,

demanding what goes away
must come back. After dark,

in the starlight and resins
I waded through the buckthorns'

scattering pins to yard's edge,
stark basin canting out to the West

and whittled alders lean as peashooters.
My grasp of the world was inelegant.

I wanted someone to be scared of me,
of my faults, my greed like unclean

sterling. My fists battered sheets
on lines. He happened to me.

I ripped up my jeans like his, splayed
across his boots so he wouldn't leave.

Slept in his closet beneath shirttails
like open-mouthed lizards. When

Uncle gave me a polka-dot bathing suit,
I wore it for weeks. If anyone came near

or yanked the spangles I screamed.
Doubt wintered over the house

like bare rafters streaming from the ends
of our ropes. I hitched myself to anything

that would keep me close. I guess that means
amen. I guess I always spent too much time

beside myself, always a little too young
to see I was a spitfire, the renegade escaped

from the shade my body made, single
white cowlick floating too close behind.

INTERIOR LIVES

Autumn already. The boxwood
out front blazes like a candy-
streaked tongue. Two cheap
columns frame the front door
no one uses. I've never seen
a boxwood so red. Shreds
of canopy heave above
like hymnbooks. Is it pain?
A rapture? A child stands
in the doorway, a girl. Nothing
behind her but blackness. Her hip
knocks to the side. I want so much
to see her face, eyelids blue
under porchlight. Her hair, brittle
as pine needles, crimson as stream
reeds. She stands there in no-
space, a pale opening in memory
while the trident of trunk strikes
up, offering a place to hang
my questions. Why must the wayward
insist on epiphany? Why this entry
into the beyond if not to mean
my instincts are correct
and my family spreads out the most
when searched for? The girl,
I believe, is my cousin. She holds
the front door open not to usher
me in, but to confirm who stands
there. Me—this bolded presence,
stealing the warmth of old
portents. I can smell the rain,
its mottled yawn as hinges bend

between me and depths of interior
lives. I was thirteen when she saw
my first blood at the family picnic,
covered my waist in her sweater
and followed me inside where I sat
still and ate saltines. Twenty
years will pass before I remember
that moment in another year
that slips away from ledgers
and never returns. Had I entered
the afternoon in its decayed breeze
where she waited in the open
door—her hand, formless, swirled
to a dense blue disc, I would not
tell her about the deaths to come,
the howling years already
startling her young face. I would not
interfere with the natural order
of things. I want to tell her
to let go of the door and step
where the day still hangs in ruby
suspension of heat and vibrancy.
Instead, she considers me the way
someone considers snowfall. The way
the passing of one body in motion
leaves parts of itself everywhere.

AFTER EVERYONE IS GONE

Behind Wagner's white barn and Wayside Park
    freight cars brake the lidded silence of sleep.
        Against the tracks, a chain-link wraps to the side
            of our duplex. Fragments of plastic bags trill

behind the concrete bench swirled in grey rose
    where scattered gravel grips the grass path toward
        the house as the birdbath and sundial slant
            in deadnettle. Lilacs warm with noon,

and in the backyard, a charred hole drops
    into some dark, opened oval where the fire bin
        burned through spring. Everything Bud and Laverne
            saved was set to flame over the hole after they died—

ticket stubs, calendars, bus tickets. They saved ledgers
    from past decades, thimbles from countries visited
        by train, stained coasters from Louisville to New Orleans.
            A tax business moved in last November,

and when there's nowhere left to go, I drive by
    and cut the engine—let the air aim my thoughts
        over all the years I'll live. I feel like saying: *Dead,*
            what do you want from me? It comes out

wrong. Along the tracks, I watch as bands of crepe
    myrtles hold nothing but black wasps bounding
        in sweeps like buttons dropping from large coats
            and behind that, saucers of diesel blow from semis

downshifting past Kroger. I hope to be cut loose too, if only
    for a while, the way erosion has blurred the flatland

clay of the riverbank miles out. There's more
    to knowing myself than haunting the backyard

as though it were a tomb. There has to be trust in an origin
    story. When I tell this one, I need to mention the sickness
        binding me to this place by blood. I know the reason—
        I'm starting to consider how when the wind

moves, all human truths outlast their own decorations.
    Even as the chimes toss, even as they heave,
        the screen door becomes an ache in the hinge
          of the jaw, silhouettes flit one place or another.

II

WHEN MY SISTER TOLD ME TO LET HER ALONE

There was a gun, the dumb luck he kept tucked in a drawer
      without a key, covered with cross-stitching of cartoon birds,
                     baby feet,
                tiny periwinkle x's
sprouting into little girls whispering
            into cupped hands. All I heard

on the phone that summer was my sister slurring
in the kitchen while cabinets slammed shut like trunks.

Whispers so her boyfriend wouldn't hear.
     As if I couldn't recognize it, the ugly in his talk,
        as if a scream wasn't buried in me somewhere, waiting

to stumble from my mouth. Even if she'd vanish
     for a second behind the clothesline into ablutions
        of yellow light, he followed like a tin can trail

scraping his frown
    up and down the dirt yard yelling her name. The river was full.

August and too much rain greened the windows of my sister's car
overgrown in weedy bluestem for over a year. It broke down.

Brakes thin, steering shot.
                 Wheel stuck in a singular stiff turn.

There was no money to fix the battery.
Tents pitched in yards. Porches gaped wide,

mattresses leaned against walls like entrepreneurs
while Louisville became the ransomed sore in her throat,

a sweltering mirage between the blur of bridges.
      Barges wore down to an oily film stretching along I-65
          like dirty fingerbones under whose steel

spins of timber lurched and turned.
      Her boyfriend was jealous and I was afraid.
          A few days in a row I waited on the end of the line

Whispering, *Walk . . . walk*
      but that afternoon I stood in a room three hundred
          miles away in my sister's hand-me-downs,

so sure I could be useful. I wanted to save her
              but that would be unhealthy. Too many times

I believed the gun in her mouth. I could see it, opening

her mouth wider, wider still. Her eyes
          skimming the ceiling, looking for the feet of angels.

She loved him. Night after night I saw her die—
          smelled the orange-shag swathed with the scent

of heady plums. Heard the piano he bought
      for her 28th birthday, shut up in the back room
she played nights with no one home singing some

motherless, nerve-split tune. A house of prayer, the heart-
engraved face of Christ
          withered to the walls. There was nothing

I could do. They were alone
          with each other and the dark day shafted slow sun

through the iron porch swing like arrests of dank air, fanning
        like money in a bankrupt home. Seed-heavy jays shook
            powerlines. Neighborhood dogs prowled the fences

and groaned in blight. In the evening, her man called
        from her phone and I was so happy, I thought my sister escaped

to the safe side of the river alone, standing tall in the sun
                with her dark hair streaked to her cheeks with good news

of escape. *Stupid-yapping-bitch* was all he said. But I always
                knew her voice was somewhere behind his chained throat,

back with the tomatoes she tended like children,
                lost in the vines
                where her heart beat slow. She loved it there.

Watched over the plants. Stepped on the stingers of dead
bees. This was new, my sister turning her back to me.

She was in love.
My hands have never been more useless—
I hated him, I hated him for making me reshape her body

in all the costumes of air. Water roped swollen vines, sludge thick.
The river hurled slick slabs, dragged what didn't want to be dragged.

THE TOP OF THE HORSESHOE CASINO

Across the state border, guitars tremble into a crowd that moves
        as though something inside it flutters and tugs. I can see
it from here, on top of the casino swamp cooler, dusk

        dipping its stung fingertips into the seed-blown bone
of me. Easy to feel undone, or in love, the kind that saws
        the air in great circles. Except through those circles

a 24-hour gun store blinks between passing tank trucks.
        This place is all ache. What with the river flanked
by pollen. What with the stage blurred. I don't know

        when I fell short of surprise, or what it means
to be serene, but I know my chew from chaw. A sign
        that the life I live and the life I arrange from dream

only proves that longing began as a storyline in the meridian
        of carnal need. No wonder my wandering repeats itself
in ways I can't forgive. I can glimpse bats fiddling through

        this lithe July mouth as always, and above the wavering
rim of song, I wait until the falsetto falls to breathe out
        the last river-scented air. Strike me past consolation.

COUNTRY MUSIC SHOW

Every Saturday, my grandmother drives her brother Bill
along the shoulder of 44 where sun falls into the low

ginkgo's and a two-lane road emerges to a bear-sized
Country Music sign, lit up by dozens of shining bulbs.

Bright like the Lord came to Shepardsville for the songs.
Inside the barn, framed photos of cowboys are hammered

into wood. Flies flit in and out of coffee cans filled
with donations. Pickles and popcorn are for sale

in a dark corner by the red curtain opening and unfurling
like a rose. Cut-outs of half notes and guitars dangle above

the stage like bats. Styrofoam cups litter the grass floor.
Everyone sits as the emcee emerges in a crimson glitter dress.

Hair, a blonde ball of spray and curl. The drum kicks in
and everyone stands for God Bless America.

The 44 Country Band jams while the emcee leaves
for a costume change. It goes on like that for a while,

memory completing its dim work over the crowd.
Nostalgia sweeping through rows the way wind lifts clothes.

Some of us out here cry during *I Will Forever Hate Roses.*
Someone floats through everyone's mind for *Goodnight Irene.*

Orbison always lifts my grandmother out of her chair,
and I leap too. Bill nods and smiles like he remembers

his wife's name is *Carolyn*. After the song reel is spent,
spectators sway into the aisle where in the glowing dark,

the curtains lower. Then the emcee sweeps into the crowd,
saying *don't you go anywhere,* one hand shaking like a tambourine.

What I'm getting at is this: my grandmother brings
her brother to the country music show every weekend.

The heartache music helps him remember who he is.
When he asks for his wife I sing, the singing almost becomes

screaming then. The feel of being hooked against the sky.
The Bill I knew once stood over a map of Louisville, spread

out on the driveway, shook a slab of sheet metal over the paper
city, and called it *Thunder Over Louisville.* I cannot explain

how I traced the rim of his sleeve in search of his hand, floating
up into the kingdom of song like a balloon. When he asks again,

the whole barn pulses with strobe light, emits clouds of dust
with every stomp, and it's either too loud or I feel too sorry

to say her name over the drum-kicks. After the horse-tailed
bow pulls across a fiddle string for the last time, after the Stetsons

are removed and the band deep-bows, the tops of their heads
like grass sat in for too long, the mic cuts out, and a great quiet

shuffles toward the heat outside. Uncle Bill leans
on my grandmother too much, forgetting his own weight

so I hold his other arm and we slow-step, follow the rhythm
of the world toward the car. It's 80 degrees after nine.

He asks if anyone remembers the way he played blackjack
in Vegas as a young man. In 1974, he gambled for so long

his back threw out. Left the casino on a gurney. As though
speaking from a mile away, he says it every Saturday.

CHECK'S, ALMOST EVERY NIGHT

The days hang under Kentucky's heavy storms.
Sky, a silver shifting smog. Rain-splotched backyards.

This is where my kin sing back to the dead.
After funerals and foreclosures, after bad news

and long labor, we prophesize over Miller Light
and three-dollar chili served in paper bowls.

My grandmother shuffles in the corner
with a man that only responds to his karaoke name.

His spurs clamber like toy trains as she spins
my way, brow-smudged and radiant:

Cash wants to take me on a cruise! After Laverne passed,
aunt Janet propped carnations along the salt-specked

tables. They drooped on thin stalks. Grandma Marilyn
unfurled Laverne's lace tablecloth, and the edges

kicked like a pair of bare legs. Another year,
uncle Don waltzed in with an unlit

candelabra, drove it down the middle of the bar,
pretending the candles were lit as evening threw down.

Tonight, James behind the bar wears a metal cross
that canters down to his belly button. Yellow rose

for a microphone, he winks a glaucous eye.
In a sideways-two step he sings a country-western

classic. Just months ago, he was on his knees
in the deep baritone of *My Achy Break-y Heart*

for my sister while she blushed in a barstool.
Not everyone likes it here. A LED neon sign

flashes orange, stuns the windows as afternoon
drunks come and go through the smoky dark.

Loose chatter forms around the best deal at Kroger.
Sudden intimacies are made. Heads lean into sweat-

lined necks that smell of Pall Mall. A *Courier-Journal*
framed on the wall calls this *the place that time forgot*.

Time wheels its wrought-iron web, redeems us all.
Meanwhile, pity-slickened years drape servicemen

along the edge of happiness yet to arrive.
They hang around drinking over red baskets

with their wives. I know I've romanticized the place,
lost in the specter of my great grandparents

doing the same shit in the Eisenhower years.
I can summon them up—they come from the hope

I was honed in, and if I lean into it
hard enough, layers of their clothes

rustle from decades ago. I could tent
the sweat-drenched shirt from Bud's back,

curl the crimp of Laverne's rosy globe of hair
around my finger and hear it set. Through

that malt-mired layer between here and there,
someone drives over the tracks going fifty.

The crack of a beer can opens at the far corner.
No one wants to go home.

THE PAST DOESN'T BURST INTO SONG LIKE IT USED TO

Too much anymore to write
into rooms that were never mine.
The afternoon assembles below
the powerlines where the Pepsi billboard,
upright and alight in its giant aluminum
can, wavers above the highway.
All there is, ever was: shadows
of branches in a windowpane
thrown across the floor, its one
watery eye. This bouquet of half-
finished history recedes, expands,
like riverbeds. Whir of beaters
downstairs before anyone opens
the door to let the trains in.

III

WHOEVER INHERITS THE FAMILY GUN HAS TO PROVE THEY CAN SHOOT

Soft as a moth's wing

                 the paper target   jolted

in my grandfather's hands, suspended against the fluorescents

like an x-ray   nothing but light. Beside us, the army boy's

ran drills, shredded targets

                   like watering roses   I entered

the shooting gallery as though it were an airplane, cement floor

a sprawl of endless scuff marks   patterns of fights   wads

of gum,   turned to dark discs.   Like limp carcasses

of dead pigs, plastic sheets

                     hung between the shooters and I,

gossamer as the bubbles I blew

                all summer   bucket and wand

if anyone looked, I'd be washed in

                green and yellow stripes

a swimmer

    gliding underwater. Targets   flitting

in the distance, stuck in prearranged postures   one caught

mid-crime, surprised. The other with a frown thin as a wick,

gun aimed straight ahead. Others,   dim outlines far off,

quiet and armless,
full of holes.
My grandfather
just wanted me to shoot.   The gun was special because it was his.

Because he kept it   nailed   to the back   of his door

by a single rusted nail. Like a pinned beetle, it jolted

by acts of imagination. I wanted to prove myself in the thesaurus

of family want—

                        crush of skin on metal   what the box fans

wouldn't silence, I could have

                        said no   thirteen, peace-sign

patch on my jeans, target rifling beyond not by wind   by rounds.

Army boys to my right, firing—how they swayed, dancing (almost)

the gloss of the clips rippled in their hands

                                divine   fire

life-ending reverberation   inviting me too.   My grandfather handed over the gun, careful as passing a baby.   *Isn't she beautiful?*

I looked at it that way, this foreign body

                this instant death,

the barrel wheeling like dandelion seeds   single yellow bullet,

a piece of candy

                  a corona   of army boys' golden shells

twitching   into the chalk circle   where I aimed

my grandfather yelling through the shots

when you pull the trigger   *it'll push back.*

                        I couldn't hear,

both of our ears covered like pilots. To my right, flush

              of camo fatigues   orange flash pulsing

through the neck of an AR-15,   a beehive of hot bullets.

To my left, loud   single   pops

            of a rifle

the recharge of which snapped up my neck,   the trigger:

pulling a sweep of hair behind a heat-scythed   sound-damaged   ear.

           Pretend the body approaches.   In the distance,

the figure flapped lightly. For a brief second I recognized

the human

                    I would tear into and when I did—

shoulder sharp with the quiver of kickback,   bullet

lodged in the ceiling (terrible shot) and what did I want?

Not the gun itself but what came after   a slit of light

                    to slip through.

ELEGY FOR MY MOTHER'S ACCENT

I've learned to live without

> the sound of crushed plums,
> the lowering of *feed me,*

I'm hongry, lodged in the gut.

Your full-sprung frown

> & penciled brow taught me to ask
> for what I want, but if I met you

before this life, a hundred degrees

outside, heat that collapses

> hydrangeas shallow & still beside
> your home on Tinkerbell, you couldn't

account for me—your *dawder.* The entwined

snare of *hayre* as you marveled

> at me in cooing song, the only blonde
> of the family—I haven't spent

one night without your rhinestone

marrow, haven't been able to wake

> without the briers of *cain't* in my head.
> Why am I still hollering

for your great, twang-lullaby

cherry-pitted inside my ear,

      it's sprouting branch?
      When your vowels stall,

I am summoned to preserve

the ever-prickling membranes,

      to sample their flammable undergrowth
      & twirl them behind my teeth

yawing into the dark to be passed onwards.

Yet we are between worlds, aren't we?

      Between syllables, elongating since
      the western summits first crested

beyond sharp turns of road

as you drove farther west,

      peeling daybreak around
      whatever *veehickle* that got you there.

Everything you said—

the color of grape skins,

      even if it was mean.
      Hard to imagine you appeared

around the scant end of spring

years & years ago, blowing

> through fields of sassafras
> & blurring mileage signs—

past the farthest reaches of county

lines, knowing you were becoming

> alchemic, part of yourself, the loot
> of my dreams now, before you thought

of leaving anything behind, least of all

the way you talk, wrung sunbeams

> over the hills, trumpet-like, spectral.
> What's left of that rebellion trills

and your haw with it. I am
at that terrible age—floundering

> for the pendulum of your phrasing
> to center like portraits so I can prove

your breath is a handful of stems

stuffed into a glass-lipped vase

> that doesn't touch bottom, but hovers,
> kelp-like in a desert sky—the movement

of which quakes in the mouth's-great

thicket, not unlike the first piano

>I learned to play, quavering flat notes
>shifting the cupboards of air you walked

through. The language you rounded up

>rolls from my tongue the way marbles
>circle hardwood floors. You forked

it to me until my heart sprung flames.
I fed you trickles of buttered light.

>I fed you my own soft name.

OPOSSUM GOSSIP

A party bus carrying the prince of Monaco
    and the Campbell's Soup boys
left Miss Kentucky stranded in the traffic
    along the corner of Brook Street.

There wasn't much to notice beneath slim pods and dripping leaves
in that shotgun section along the rails.
    Trash spattered across the streets.

Plastic bags churned in the curbs like whitewashed sails.

We sat in the yard all afternoon watching the trains
work their way past the back of the house.

Churchill Downs wasn't a mile's walk past girlie signs and pawnshops.
But in Bud's house, threaded flowers stitched the small couches in swirls.

Thick yellow curtains twisted the light dry. A claustrophobic nest.
The old smell of fuel.

Bud pulled on his sleeves, rolled and unrolled the newspaper,
underlined horse names, and circled jockey stripes.

My sister breathed hard, braided my hair drum-tight.
I didn't tell her how it hurt. Everyone placed their bets in the family pot,

a dollar each to wager. That gnat-fizzing evening
we all lost our bets, except for Bud.

When Miss Kentucky strolled in, she sat between Bud
and I at the supper table.

She came through with her big hat and her high heels
and looked that house up and down. I tried to explain just who she was

and what she was doing at his table, but he didn't understand.
I could barely hear the TV in the next room.

By the fifth race, all the windows were wide open. Buds Will
was taped to the refrigerator, reinforced by magnets of Pope Francis.

There weren't enough chairs, so my mother moved to the rocker.
Aunt Janet apologized everybody ate the hot-pie but offered
cold pork chops and Miller Light.

Miss Kentucky never took off her hat.
That whole night, she never took off that hat.

I don't know if I ever saw who she was
or if she saw us for who we really were either—wild and ravenous.

When Miss Kentucky ate everyone sat up straighter.
Bud cried again. *That's a good song,* he said except there was no song,
only the push of plates across lace.

Funny how grief comes back unknown.

It was the last derby of Bud's life, before the year of triple crowns
and California Chrome.
One more year and everything he had in that house would be in boxes.

I loved my mother for bringing us back, for sitting in the corner
beneath a straw hat watching them watch the beauty queen

come in and out of their lives as frequently as the L&N
that rattled the glass of that house for years.

And the opossums in the catalpas chewed their leaves in the ditches
and watched us say hello and goodbye every year since.

The way my mother sees it: everyone here is all talk. Cruel gossip.
Until they are set loose, she says, *then they are the most beautiful things.*

BEHIND THE RAILROAD

The patriarch stares from his workshop where Old Forester
bottles blink into the day's pageantry of sunlight. He glares

from the plaster on which he hangs in portraiture, bowling ball
in hand, our whole world made edgeless, younger

than I am now, unaware of us stacking his decks of cards,
stained kings sacrament to the kind of luck that cannot be

willed but cambers up, makes itself known, gives nothing.
I touch a water mark on a box of cards that appears

the most warped, penny-sized, though whatever ink-blot
it's become is just the blank square of a photo removed

from a wall after years of no use. Bud's stop sign, slantwise
by the garage, takes root. Capital letters faded from years

of wear with the testimony: *You are trespassing*, is painted
in sweeps of white-out across the wide scrap of its octagon.

Everything my grandmother cannot throw away she saves
for me. When did my chest become a dam, that house,

the lurching wake of my blood? Against the shed, Bud's sign
slants—a tilted head, considering my trespasses. In a while

hundreds of glass insulators, horseshoes and barrels of nails
will clatter across carport symmetry. It's still April.

Last night's rain spills into the garage, gathers in places
made empty. In soft dents of earth, a pool shallows

into a pocket of cement. My grandmother's arm ripples
in its reflection, steadying the stop sign from falling.

Dandelions swell up in preordained orbits where shreds
of birch flip in breezes I wish I could hold steady. Spiderwebs

battered by morning storms, coagulate in corner's like choirs
rising for song as the garage rouses yellowjackets

from its cold. Times like these, I think of the places
he shouldered the stop sign. How deep did it's hole-

punched tongue plunge into the earth's crumbling
gums? Everything my grandmother, innkeeper

of his artifacts, cannot throw away she saves
for me. Suppose daughter-hood claims a girl.

Often enough, we've returned together and alone, re-lived
the parties, swirled highballs in 1983 winner

glasses and shot back to another year of scorn
incarnadine. This time, it's me who wanders out

to scrawl the chalk across the driveway
where our toy horses *circle, circle, circle.*

HOW TO LIVE FOREVER

For my grandfather

You imagined flocks of finches rising from radial canals of dark. They came to you the same slow way you spread your hands along your jeans. They carried you over the ocean. There is no ocean in Kentucky, so the image remains an idea, a practice in council with God. In the complicated stream of worry, you whisper to let all preoccupations of my mind be carried by starlings or egrets or herons beyond the water too. *Don't fight it when they come, either.* Let them come in their hundreds, surging applause from the willow-strung muck. Let them come with their blue bodies bellowing. Loud and riven and familiar they'll come to the mind's tortured wake, its lit wax of thought. Tell me about no longer being bound by this world. *Shapeless,* you say. Yesterday, I read about sharks in Mammoth Cave. Fragments of tooth and bone found in the deepest canals. Did you dream of oceans flowing over this damp soil smelling of ethanol, grandfather? Sharks in Kentucky and your paper-thin shirt is still warm from the iron. As though posed for a painting, your reflection on the bus is a vanishing mirage marred by leafless sky. Time goes far beyond what I can see, so I wait in the place where moths shed powdery lines. Along Watterson Expressway where the road forks, I do what you say, and let the day's shadows drift where dark wingbeats drive up beyond these hemlocks and cattle cars.

IV

15 ORIGIN STORIES

I always thought my ancestors must have wanted
too much, in the end, that black star blooming—

                    Kentucky beyond the valley,
                    its secular dusk
                    too low to see the skylarks flight
from branch to branch
over those hundred miles, unmoved
at the trail and in determination, like hallucinations,
                the travelers ambling together, not away,

but toward something I've never allowed for.

                  • • •

O, the places I have called them up.

Martin's Fork, Sugar Run, the Ohio—
log cabins split by axe, plaster made of lime, mud,

animal hair. Steeples of smoke piercing into hide-
burned evenings. The weathered fabric

of women's dresses swirled by time and heat, hung
from the branches of beeches, a landscape of deflated air.

                  • • •

My grandfather gets lost in the fragments—forgets names,
our origins distilled to a familiar ache, their handprints lodged
              into our minds like a fungus, one crenelated fact.

. . .

Today, he tells me our ancestors crossed the Cumberland Gap
    with Daniel Boone.

Once, there was a ridgeline flickering its saps.
Once, circles of flies vined their tripwires over our footfall.

. . .

I tell myself an old face won't fade like paint in old light.
I tell myself they were good people.

I imagine my ancestors covering their eyes
from sun flecks on the river's surface, before their bodies became
crescents against the enormous autumnal hills.

. . .

Over the floodway's blurting sleet,
                        the lowlands that swirl
                        into lakes of gar parcels
the secret of life into me, the family alto, spurting

                        this pillage and strife and blunder.

. . .

I feel most descendant when I remember this,

        when I force myself to cleave open our story
        until I become engine-heavy, churning the current

against the sawyers of our drifting history.

・・・

I thought I controlled my blunders,
                                my tendency to pry at openings
within my inheritances, but within the heirloom
                                of my genetics—the acoustics
of our coming and going, a pearl
                                of permanency hardens.

・・・

If I think hard enough they appear
before me in their rags and worn faces etched with distance.

O, dawn's veneer of stars, allow me
the origin of Springs volatile headwaters.

I could beg for their wild melt if I had a mind to.

・・・

I try to figure how Boone, age thirty-two when he crossed the gap,
the same age I am now, didn't die. I will never know if he worried
about a sense of direction. What amusements floated place to place
beneath a red moonscape. Pawpaw's mistaken for scarecrows.
All I hold true, more or less, is what my grandfather articulates—

・・・

                Daniel, tell me the nights,
        leaf-frail and mica-thin, were torn

        with distant triggers, bullets chewing holes
through trophied hides. Tell me the mineral-glint

of cliffsides were mistaken for a bright
beyond while above, constellations projected

their own country across your desire-wrecked
body, lanterned there, skulking.

• • •

I know little. I wane,
        seized by people suspended
by purpose in a time long gone.

Nothing can change that,
        they are flinders across the canebrakes of yesterday

and not this rain-swept air
        above the Wendy's or K-Mart's of Kentucky.

• • •

None of it was theirs.

• • •

My grandfather says it as prophecy—
        always his *to make a long story short*
while we look to the caravan
        of eighteen wheelers, gunning
out of town like money kings
        crossing our nocturnal pulpit
of existence, their shifting gears,
        a solitude chambered within
the river shoal's bluest year.

TO THE OHIO RIVER VALLEY

The city wakes in pairs
of crossed fingers. Steel

bridges string ellipses
        over the river's blubbering mouth,

deep as a baritone. The current turns
and golden flax shifts in its wind-shattered shell.

                        It hears me coming through

the liturgy of Spring. Trains ring bottles
of milk in the refrigerator and laundry
                        drips into the flowers. Like bad teeth,

blinds lilt and lodge behind windows.
I heard it too—

this blunt life overfilled us with belief.

If that cloud-heavy dusk, its ore-laden strata strung
                        like an embroidered purse,
                        heavy with idleness

and gossip, extends an arthritic hand,
calls me home, who will sit with me? The one

who has refused truces with the wheel
                        of memory—cleave me

instead, open-mouthed, loosed
from my own story so I may drink

                        the spring-fed revelation
                                of returning.

PACKED CARS

Sixty-five summers ago
     my grandfather clutches the trunk
     of the Pontiac, defeated

and circumspect. The moving truck
     adjacent like a pop-up church,
     hand-painted saints glued to the dash

bless the windshield, beatific and exact.
     By the trunk, my grandfather
     tilts his shaved head

downward at an angle reminiscent
     of light through glass. I wish
     I could saddle up to the sharp baking-

soda smell of my grandfather,
     his exhaustion, my pronunciation. Open
     a hole inside memory's rising chest

and I will tuck myself inside my grandmother's
     posture, her shoulders stooped
     as handlebars lodged into the front yards

of Frankfort Avenue, the space
     around her perfumed by the stiff
     alcohol of a single rose when she reaches

for my hand. Only wasps blast
     through the front grill where my grandparents
     face each other now. Behind them,

shapes of a life hide beneath a canvas
blanket secured to the bed by ropes.

• • •

I've been trying to hold all this under
a magnifying glass, the serviceberries

crush along the sidewalks of my mother's
girlhood that began beneath these thaw-

wet willows and the hard static
of radio signals naming the dead

from Saigon. What frequency,
if any, sung distant death reports

while they caravanned the thirty-six
miles to Saint Louis, cramped

and moonless, the only direction
I know they are still fastened behind

the blacked-out future
I am bound to.

• • •

It's all I have to bring today
            Dickinson wrote, and now I repeat—

if I could just speak to them in 1963, holler
            over the cicadas' one sharpening

story, their dormitory of swallowed heat
        aswarm with impending diminishment,

instead of watching the lakes
        my eyes make over the begats

before me. It's all I have to bring—
        theirs is the season I crush against me.

• • •

When I was five, I helped my uncle move
from our house to his apartment. I craned

my neck around from inside his Ranger
as old boxes shifted in the bed, softened

tape ripping up thick strips. The boxes
opened like tulips, loose and mute

along I-25. Neon shorts and Looney-
Toons tank tops mottled the meridians.

In memory number one, he ran
across traffic slinging his clothes

back into his sunburned arms.
In memory number two, we leave

the shirts spiraling behind us,
our own chaos spattered over

the windshields of rush hour.
In reality, I sat in the truck,

amazed by the jerk of silhouettes,
of one life winnowing and another—

• • •

They are leaving the state in their fold out maps,
            in the headscarves and overheated backseats

of the Ohio River Valley. If ever there was a time
for the yellowwoods to droop—
                        here they are, faceless
                        beneath the bulb of canopy.

• • •

My mother, three, wears a white dress
                        and black church shoes, erases
into a streak of light. Her ankle-high

                        socks fade into straps of shoes
the size of scissors, clattering over
                        gravel into the car held ajar.

She won't remember the drive
                        or the year itself. Still,
I want her to stay in the frame

                        long enough for me to explain
how it's almost May and gone
                        are the jeweled oaks hanging
from the bugle's long delay.

MAN WALKING HOME WITH GOOD NEWS

In the photo, my great grandfather
pauses with arms crossed as swaths

of roses ambush the sides of the frame,
grow toward his eyes. Years under

the emerald spires set Bud Lattis' purpose—
to live so close to risk he made a home

against its domed applause. After
the cellophane of his dying, after

the flowers and cards stopped, after
the not-watched derbies and my not

coming back, the guilt raked
the animal blood within and left me

shamed. After all that passed,
he entered my life one May evening,

young and slender again, in his pleated
slacks and leather jacket. It's the winner's

circle, 1959. His crooked smile beams
upward in the fragrant afternoon

while the roses clatter behind
like teacups. You're thinking

of dawn's capacity for renewal,
you're thinking there were never

enough years for a man
to dawdle outside the track

for nothing if not cash money.
Let's not pretend this isn't about

the money. Then again, this is a man
who learned to lose the way

a river reverses, years of patience
until loss felt like a welcome. See

the horses leave the paddock
before emerging to the track,

restrained, paraded? He, too,
tried to pull back the inevitable

growth of his own children. The sharp
temper of his girls, the back-talk

encircling his legs. He reaches out
for my grandmother's hand,

and it's the same palm that approached
Hidden Talent the year before,

her cold nose reading the map
of lines etched across his skin. His laugh

made of gravel and clover calming
his girls' tantrums, the same race-day

chatter that filled his mind speaking
to Lori-El through the TV

in 1957. His boys, eager and allusive
in their competition for love, he knew

to meet with indifference. No
favorites, an obvious rule. He couldn't

tell his children beneath the trumpet
of every race the prayer he made

to the God of Chance, but a gentle
sweep of pomade hung in his hair

like a buckle, and by nine in the evening,
the world he lost would go back to dream,

back to the walled-in obedience
where filthy diners and gas

stations burned their last half-off
offerings, and beckoned. I'll be there

too—inside the earth's pure
exhaustion that remembers my name,

gives off the perfume of tobacco
and fuel. As the first cars groan down

Central, laden with beer cans
and cigarettes, urged toward the city

that belongs to no one, the stars
slowly burn out above, becoming

the blue I'll eventually wake to,
accepting the life I already have.

Not the daydreams lasting decades, not
the unfulfilled promises to myself

I didn't keep, couldn't have kept
anyway, because that would mean

what's become of them lives on
as this roar in my mind never

learning to ask for what it wants.
Bud's one dream: home

with a winning trifecta, his hand
aloft to halt the Lincoln racketing

into the driveway as his sons, behind
the headlights, spilled themselves

from the chassis, side-stepping
into the starting gates of the open door

while the gambling world fell
toward sleep's broken compass.

COOKING LESSONS

I grip the bed rails shaped
like a lotto ticket, the garden
her mattress became—stained
gardenias bloom large. The afternoon

has a voice like rubber tires filled
with cement, but I wait for the crush
that comes after my exhale, look
for what I can recognize—the art

on her walls, my great-grandfather's
sketches of old German towns,
the geometry angular, each façade
like the face of a cousin. Don't ask how

it is that I came to beg. It began
with a rousing, the meadow
of her kitchen, heat-specked
and wrecked by winter sunlight,

golden as a sunflower soaking in a glass
of warm beer. Those days before
I knew patience was a burn,
she poked forks into the tops

of loaves and cakes, leaned
into the lustrous heat of the stove.
Always bent over the sink where the clangs
of Buehner Sheet Metal rang

over the pawn shops and bars
to the track's charcoaled expanses,

twisting black beyond the river.
Always the hole in her right

hand where, as a girl, her palm
pressed against the flamed
metal of a cast-iron, searing
a pea-sized welt into the skin-line

meant for longevity. I can tell you
the shape the burn made
but not whether she ever stopped
feeling it. I can tell you there

were nights the backyard freights
felt like a cavalry marching to war,
but not if the sting of girlhood
stigmata gave her the feel for lightning

in the air. Whenever she held
out her palm, ushered me in,
I tried to squint through, as though
the hole in her hand was torrid

and hot like night in our imagined
Louisville where everyone knew
how to live, where dawn's
pollen-spoked eye withered

the impatiens fighting across the back
half-acre of the property. If only
she explained laboring this way, I may
have believed we could go on

licking icing from our fingers
in the diminishing age of gas stoves.

Come summer, I'll question
what shortening dusted from workers'

hands taught me such grit. How baking
soda globs on to whatever milk
sours in the fridge, is its own respite
for change. My boxed yellow

cake mix. My tooth-pick taste
test. When I was a girl, my hands
fanned inside the blue rims
of her glass bowls as though

reaching into the mouth of a cave.
This fits inside every morning
I wake to: what is it she is telling me
with her cursive, her ¼ cup

less water? If the batter thins,
the topping sinks. Still tastes
good. This life caves low in the chest
where we tried too hard.

MY GREAT GRANDMOTHER CROSSES THE RIVER

Her body is beholden
        to the decayed riverbank,
right arm bent against the ferry's
        stout frame. A mile out,

the opposite shore smears
        in dank expanse, sycamores
dense in the owl–dark
        of June. In the foreground,

heat radiates from fenders
        of Chevys parked
in rows of three on the deck.
        There is a sun so warm

you mistake it for sleep.
        How easily the photographer's
gaze opens a hole in me. My great
        grandfather, collector

of ease, architect
        of routine, captured
her best in the language
        of her skepticism. I believe

her thoughts tilt toward
        the unknowable. Could
it be me, a chance
        reckoning with the future?

Here she is wholly
        present, spirited

as a child, pink
           headscarf tied in the shape

of a bell, so bright
           it rings. Her frown
deepens to a singular
           point and I know

what she would say,
           Is this not enough? She'd be right,
I've spent enough time
           peering through albums

until I see myself staring
           back as if I didn't know
my own regrets—memorabilia
           I don't recognize,

family that doesn't know me.
           I'm where the self finds
another name, two generations away.
           Can the heart be so sick

with yearning it cleaves blood-
           fat clots from burled arteries?
Suppose I tell her where I am,
           how leaving the country meant

paying off my debt. I'm still
           out here giving what I have
to these jarred-in mornings
           of stream frogs and dust.

Suspended, not unlike her,
           above an eventuality clouded

and stirred by current. That I've never
     come back. What then?

If I tell her it's loneliness
     that raised me, will it mean
I can come home
     through buckeye-sought

roots, through the wild rye
     and dropseed, spread against
the night like thinning
     hair? Beneath the silt-heavy

willows, warm music
     from the eastern shore
warps forward like an under-
     bite. Already, I sense myself

on the other side, furred with sweat.
     The ferry pulls beneath
the winding of insects. Forever, the sputtering
     of engines rev in the wrong gear.

IN THE COUNTRY OF HARD LIFE AND ROSEBUDS

It keeps happening, missed turns—
another reason to believe myself
a fraud here, belonging to a people
I can't find my own way to. Not long
ago, my sister joked about painting *lawyer*
for hire over her windows for some work,
but walk through Bernheim forest
as the larks lift from ancient oaks
and there is a vocation. Same
how Pearls Food Mart, known
as "just ok" fills your tank by the Biker's
Church where AA meetings are advertised:
Perfect People Unwelcome. Across
is the barbershop brushed over
in thick paint spelling—*and taxes*—Oh,
how I lingered at that intersection,
laughed to myself, tried to tune
the radio to any station, dial stuck
on static.
                    I'm supposed to visit
my grandmother today, it's why
I ask to drive the old Toyota
into town. My sister calls out
of work, the dog rips a squeaker
from a toy duck along the fence
line and beyond that, the Grill
and Chill closes early where years ago,
at a less responsible age, we ate

jumbo pizza and lifted plastic cups
from the trash instead of paying
the seventy-five cents. Sister,
we were quick as engine ignitions
to love. Now, I'm a woman palsied
by her own going, softened
into the heat of this single-lane
where my hand grips the wheel
and a paper with your directions
sends me north. It flits in the seat
as a fish would, seeking a way out,
or back into what it knows. I have
returned (not often enough) to these pastures
and limestone bluffs screaming through
years I've laid waste to.

                       I know myself
by what I cannot leave and leave
anyway. Already, I miss your rolling
laugh, your TMJ sharpened
to exclamation. I listen
for your body's articulations,
a hundred clicks of sheet music
swept over a hardwood floor
semaphored by leaves
scraping the porch of silence. Sister,
you always forgave me, why—
knowing a faint depression bid me
into another summer? The flicker
of my coming back—how I said:
Let me be born again. Leave

Mt. Washington and the pang
of yearning, its overturned
hull, is begged back toward
a good living, a rubber band
easing its tension. Then I will
forever be traveling alongside
the fencerows of Bullitt County,
forever in a spring that never comes.